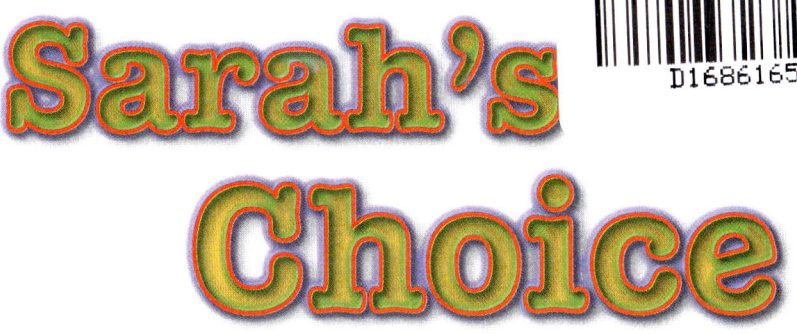

Sarah's Choice

by Ellen Chapman

illustrated by Freddie Levin

Editorial Offices: Glenview, Illinois • Parsippany, New Jersey • New York, New York
Sales Offices: Needham, Massachusetts • Duluth, Georgia • Glenview, Illinois
Coppell, Texas • Ontario, California • Mesa, Arizona

Every effort has been made to secure permission and provide appropriate credit for photographic material. The publisher deeply regrets any omission and pledges to correct errors called to its attention in subsequent editions.

Unless otherwise acknowledged, all photographs are the property of Scott Foresman, a division of Pearson Education.

Photo locators denoted as follows: Top (T), Center (C), Bottom (B), Left (L), Right (R), Background (Bkgd)

Illustrations by Freddie Levin

ISBN: 0-328-13340-X

Copyright © Pearson Education, Inc.

All Rights Reserved. Printed in the United States of America. This publication is protected by Copyright, and permission should be obtained from the publisher prior to any prohibited reproduction, storage in a retrieval system, or transmission in any form by any means, electronic, mechanical, photocopying, recording, or likewise. For information regarding permission(s), write to: Permissions Department, Scott Foresman, 1900 East Lake Avenue, Glenview, Illinois 60025.

7 8 9 10 V0G1 14 13 12 11 10 09 08

It was a warm summer day, and the sky was clear and blue. Sarah thought it was a perfect day to ask her new friend, Julia, to play. Julia had just moved in down the street.

Sarah ran to Julia's house and rang the doorbell. Julia came to the door, and Sarah motioned for her to come outside. "Would you like to run through my sprinkler today?" Sarah asked.

Julia smiled with excitement. "If my mom says it's OK, I'll be right over!"

A few minutes later, Sarah's screen door slammed shut. Julia had arrived!

"Girls, play outside awhile," said Sarah's mom. "I have to call the gardener about the new bushes. There is lemonade for you when you come in. Later, we'll bake a special treat!"

Sarah and Julia dashed outside. At last they were running through the cold spray!

After playing awhile, the girls shivered and grabbed their towels. They ran inside. "Let's have our lemonade," Sarah said.

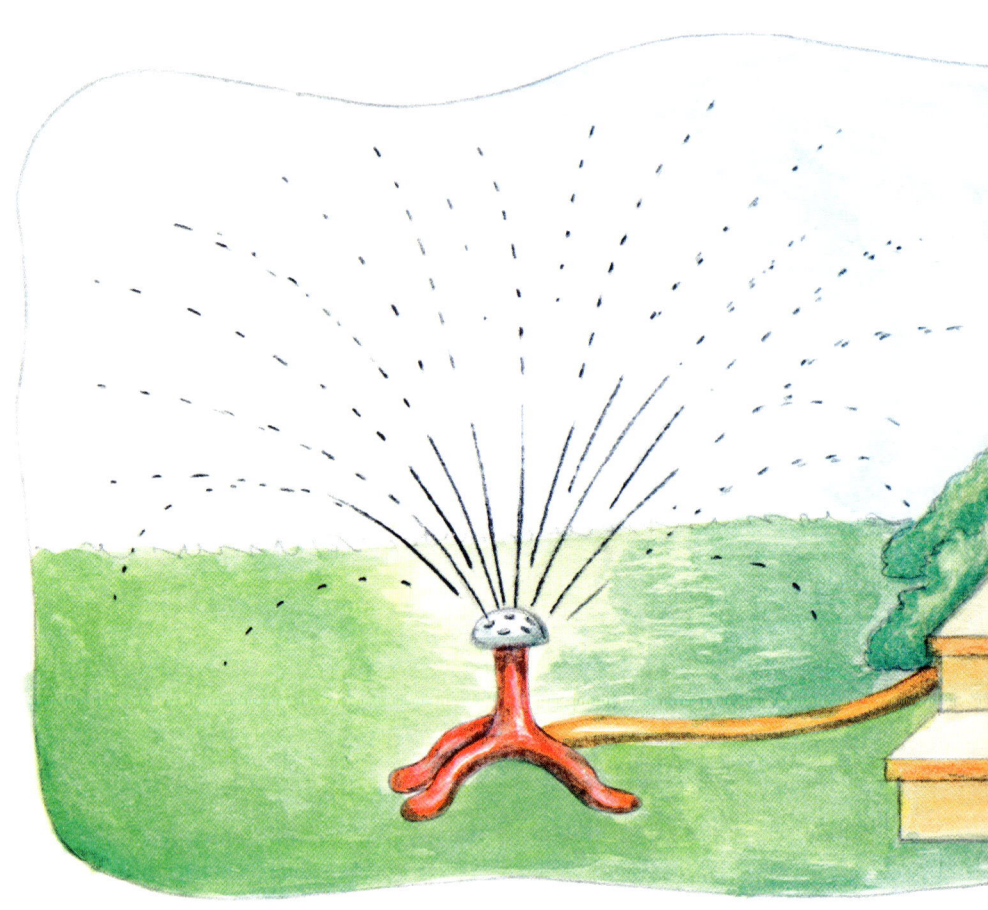

The two friends sat on the porch and talked about their summer plans. Suddenly Sarah asked, "Are you hungry, Julia? I am! Let's change and get something to eat."

In the kitchen Julia was shocked to see her friend take a carton of blueberries from the refrigerator. "Shouldn't we ask your mom first?" Julia asked.

But Sarah chose not to ask her mom. She washed the berries and put them in a bowl.

"Try some," Sarah said, as she took a handful of berries. "Blueberries are good for you. And they're yummy!"

Julia took a handful. Within a few minutes the girls had eaten every berry in the bowl.

Sarah's mom came into the kitchen as they were washing the bowl. "Girls, are you ready to make a blueberry cake? It's Sarah's favorite dessert."

"Oh, no!" Sarah cried, with sadness in her voice. "We ate all the blueberries! I wish I had asked you first, Mom! I'm sorry."

"I'm sorry, too, Sarah," said her mom. "I was looking forward to baking with you and Julia. I hope you have learned an important lesson today. If you have, that's something to be happy about after all. We'll make a blueberry cake the next time that Julia visits!"

"Thanks, Mom," Sarah said, happily.

A Harvest Celebration

Every year in late August a small town in the state of Maine celebrates. Can you guess what this celebration is about? It's about blueberries!

Maine is famous for sweet-tasting, low-bush blueberries. The berries grow wild on vines that are close to the ground. Each August, men, women, and teenagers harvest the berries by raking them. They use a scoop-shaped rake that catches and holds the berries until it is full.

The citizens of Machias, Maine, hold their two-day blueberry festival when the harvest is finished. There is a fish fry supper with blueberry pie for dessert, a children's parade, a blueberry pancake breakfast, a road race, and a craft fair. The townspeople also perform in a special play that's all about blueberries!

Blueberries are an important crop and a special tradition in the state of Maine!